LARRY CORYELL'S
POWER JAZZ GUITAR

LARRY CORYELL'S POWER JAZZ GUITAR

EXTENDING YOUR CREATIVE REACH

Backbeat
Books
San Francisco

Published by Backbeat Books
600 Harrison Street, San Francisco, CA 94107
www.backbeatbooks.com
Email: books@musicplayer.com
An imprint of the Music Player Network
United Entertainment Media, Inc.
Publishers of *Guitar Player* and musicplayer.com

Distributed to the book trade in the U.S. and Canada by
Publishers Group West, 1700 Fourth Street, Berkeley, CA 94710

Distributed to the music trade in the U.S. and Canada by
Hal Leonard Publishing, P.O. Box 13819, Milwaukee, WI 53213

Cover Design by Richard Leeds
Front Cover Photo by Bob Berg
Text Design and Composition by Chris Ledgerwood

06 07 08 09   5 4 3 2

CONTENTS

To Daisaku Ikeda,
for teaching me how to teach

FOREWORD

BY BILL FRISELL

Growing up in Denver, Colorado, I wasn't exposed to much "jazz" music. In high school I was lucky enough to find a Wes Montgomery record and was immediately hooked—he became my first big jazz guitar hero. In the summer of 1968, the Newport Jazz Festival brought a big concert to town. Wes was to be one of the featured artists, along with Cannonball Adderley, Dionne Warwick, Thelonious Monk, and the Gary Burton Quartet. I hadn't heard much about these other people; I just wanted to see Wes Montgomery, so I got my ticket right away.

Unfortunately, he passed away before the concert, but I decided to go anyway. I'd never heard of the Gary Burton Quartet (Gary Burton, vibes; Larry Coryell, guitar; Steve Swallow, bass; Bob Moses, drums), and I wasn't prepared for how my mind was going to be blown. I couldn't believe what Larry Coryell was playing—I'd never heard anything like it.

This music left a huge impression on me, and it became a kind of blueprint for what I've tried to do. If I had to point to just one guitar player who opened up the doors, showed what was possible, laid the groundwork—it would be Larry Coryell. His playing had so much finesse and intelligence, and at the same time complete abandon and danger. It was connected to the past but jumped off into the unknown. Courageous.

I went out and got every record I could find with him on it—Chico Hamilton, all the Gary Burton records, the Count's Rock Band with Steve Marcus, Herbie Mann's *Memphis Underground*, and Larry's own records. I wore out *Spaces*, which had Larry and John McLaughlin together—wow! It was an exciting time in music. You could see the whole history move forward with each new recording.

Larry Coryell keeps growing. Today his playing is deeper and better than ever. It's so inspiring. I'm thankful he's around, and I'm looking forward to spending time with this new book. It's rich with information—each page generates more and more possibilities. *Extending Your Creative Reach* is an apt title. It will stretch your ears, your mind, your hands.

Thank you, Larry.

INTRODUCTION

In my journey as a musician, I often remember a remark of the late guitar master Gabor Szabo, who heard me when I was about 20 years old. "Larry," he said, "remember, the music comes first, the instrument second."

This was very good advice, but what exactly does it mean in practice? When I improvise on the guitar, I often have to choose whether to take a risk and go for something off the wall, or to play it a little safer (more musical?) and simpler. I haven't always known what to do in certain points in a performance—should I be the virtuoso or the minimalist?

I love to hear virtuosity, not only in jazz but in classical, folk, or any other form, because of the respect I have for the work that goes into learning how to get around on one's instrument. At the same time, I am always knocked out when I hear just one great note, one creative phrase, or a deft use of space from a player in the heat of battle—an expression that reaches below the noisy superficiality of life into the deeper consciousness.

Stripped down to its basic definition, music is a combination of sound and silence. It requires tremendous practice to find the right balance of those elements while playing in tune and with grace, good timing, and taste. I think I developed whatever taste I have more through being told how to use silence than how to use sound. As Miles once said to me, "Never finish a phrase."

With the guitar, we can improvise or play compositions using chords, accompaniment, melody, and so on. Combine all those choices with the rich harmonic and rhythmic variety that is found in jazz, and you have situations where complex musical decisions have to be made instantly but tastefully. To succeed in those situations, you have to listen to many great players who know how to work with the harmony and the time in a reactive mode—as if from instinct. And you need to practice the tricky situations so you are capable of playing the right phrases in the moment. This book provides some exercises and ideas to help you do that.

It's really hard to improvise well in jazz, I believe, especially on guitar. It's great to play on modes and vamps and just improvise with one scale, but if we combine modes and scales with imaginative rhythms, we can create extended improvisations that take a listener to a universe that exists only in art. And if we find new ways of playing with nonguitar sources and with new and different techniques, we can retain the beauty of what makes it jazz in the first place and add an indefinable but real quality called our own voice. That's what this book wants to help you do.

Good luck.

— Larry Coryell

ON THE CD

Track 1:   Tuning

Track 2:   Ex. 1.1 with pick, quarter-note = 88

Track 3:   Ex. 1.1 fingerstyle, quarter-note = 80

Track 4:   Ex. 1.2 with pick, quarter-note = 88

Track 5:   Ex. 1.2 fingerstyle, quarter-note = 80

Track 6:   Ex. 1.3, quarter-note = 88

Track 7:   Ex. 1.4, quarter-note = 88

Track 8:   Ex. 2.1

Track 9:   Ex. 2.1, Guitar 2 only

Track 10:   Ex. 2.2

Track 11:   Ex. 2.2, Guitar 2 only

Track 12:   Ex. 2.3

Track 13:   Ex. 2.3, Guitar 2 only

Track 14:   Ex. 2.4

Track 15:   Larry explains Examples 2.1–2.3; to be played straight through

Track 16:   Examples 2.1–2.3, Guitar 2 only

Track 17:   Larry talks about Ex. 2.5

Track 18:   The "Slonimsky Ex. 3" scale

Track 19:   Larry introduces the G♭ jazz minor scale

Track 20:   G♭ jazz minor scale, from *F*

Track 21:   Larry introduces the 1-plus-2 scale

Track 22:   The 1-plus-2 scale starting from *F*

Track 23:   Larry introduces the whole-tone scale

Track 24:   The whole-tone scale starting from *F*

Track 25:   Larry introduces the whole-tone chromatic scale

Track 26:   The whole-tone chromatic scale

Track 27:   Larry introduces the whole-tone chromatic variation

Track 28:   The whole-tone chromatic variation in 3/4

Track 29:   The melody of "Blues for Yoshihiro Hattori," normal tempo

Track 30:   The melody of "Blues for Yoshihiro Hattori," slow tempo

Track 31:   Ex. 3.3, melody scales for "Blues for Yoshihiro Hattori"; Larry explains and plays the *Gdim9* scale

Track 32:   Larry explains and plays the 1-plus-2 scale from *E* with passing tones

Track 33:   Larry explains and plays the 2-plus-1 scale from *C#* with passing tones, then the 1-plus-2 starting from *D*

Track 34:   Larry explains and plays the *G* whole-tone scale with passing tones.

Track 35:   Larry explains and plays the 2-plus-1 from *F#* with passing tone

Track 36:   Ex. 3.4, solo transcription of "Blues for Yoshihiro Hattori," normal tempo

Track 37:   Ex. 3.4, solo transcription of "Blues for Yoshihiro Hattori," slow tempo

Track 38:   Backing track for "Blues for Yoshihiro Hattori" to accompany the solo transcription or your own solo

Track 39:   Ex. 3.5, altered m7♭5 improvisation

Track 40:   Ex. 3.5, Guitar 2 only

Track 41:   Ex. 3.6, m7♭5–7#5–min7–7#11

Track 42:   Ex. 3.6, Guitar 2 only

Track 43:   Ex. 3.7, m7♭5 to m7♭5

Track 44: Ex. 3.7, Guitar 2 only

Track 45: Ex. 3.8, m7♭5–7♭9–7♯11, with lead-in

Track 46: Ex. 3.8, Guitar 2 only

Track 47: Ex. 4.1, literal comping

Track 48: Ex. 4.2, "out" comping

Track 49: Ex. 4.3, literal solo

Track 50: Ex. 4.4, "out" solo

Track 51: Ex. 4.5, excerpt from "Pedals and Suspensions," ensemble recording

Track 52: Larry introduces the guitar part from "Pedals and Suspensions"

Track 53: Ex. 4.5, guitar only

Track 54: Ex. 4.6, Guitar 2 only

Track 55: Ex. 4.6, Guitar 1 only

Track 56: Ex. 4.6, Guitar 2 plus Guitar 1

Track 57: Ex. 5.1, intro to "Turkish Coffee 2000"

Track 58: Ex. 5.2, first three choruses, "Turkish Coffee 2000"

Track 59: Ex. 5.3, fourth chorus, "Turkish Coffee 2000"

Track 60: Ex. 5.4, "Transparence," normal tempo

Track 61: Ex. 5.4, "Transparence," slow tempo; each click = three eighth-notes

MUSIC CREDITS

Examples 3.1–3.4, "Blues for Yoshihiro Hattori" by Larry Coryell, Coryell Publishing, from *Count's Jam Band* track 6, courtesy ToneCenter Records

Example 4.5, "Pedals and Suspensions" by Larry Coryell, Coryell Publishing, from *Count's Jam Band* track 4, courtesy ToneCenter Records

Examples 5.1–5.3, "Turkish Coffee" by Larry Coryell, Coryell Publishing, from *Inner Urge*, HCD 7064 track 8, courtesy High Note Records

Example 5.4, from "Transparence" by Larry Coryell, Coryell Publishing, from *The Coryells* track 12, courtesy Chesky Records

CHAPTER 1

INTERVALS
AND ARPEGGIOS

Befor we begin looking at ways to
expand and improve your solos, I want you to play some exercises to develop
your technique and, at the same time, attune your ear to intervals. Many pro-
gressions in our music use the fourth and fifth intervals: a II–V–I progression in
C major, for example, might go from *Dm7*, down a fifth (or up a fourth) to *G7*,
and then up a fourth (or down a fifth) to resolve to the *C* major chord. At the
same time, a lot of modern chords use stacks of fourths, which can be also
understood as descending fifths reversed. For instance, if you take *C* at the 8th
fret, 1st string; *F* at the 6th fret, 2nd string; and *B♭* at the 8th fret, 4th string, and
reverse the octaves of the *C* and *B♭*, you get a stack of fourths: *C, F, B♭*.

Before we get started, you can use CD Track 1 to tune up.

EASY FIFTHS EXERCISES

"Easy Fifths Exercise 1" (**Ex. 1.1;** Tracks 2–3) is an arpeggio of four ascending
fifths intervals. In measures 1–10, the arpeggios ascend chromatically from *E* to
C♯. Measures 11–16 take the same arpeggio up again, this time in whole steps.
Measures 17–21 return to the beginning and go up this time in minor thirds.

The final arpeggio, measure 21, makes a small variation and uses an artificial harmonic for the *G♯* on the third beat. To play an artificial harmonic, use

Ex. 1.1   **Easy Fifths Exercise 1**

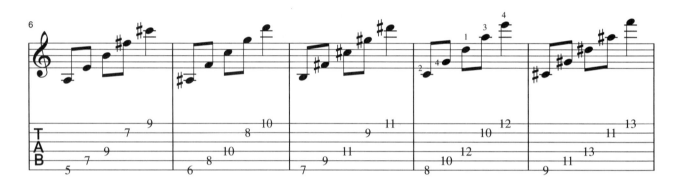

the tip of your right-hand 1st finger to touch the string 12 frets above the note your left hand is holding, while you pluck the string with the pick held between the thumb and 2nd finger. [Throughout this book, right hand = picking hand, left hand = fretting.] In the case of this *G♯,* your left hand is at the 9th fret of the 2nd string, so the "touch point" 12 frets higher is the 21st fret.

The *E* harmonic at the end is normally played as a natural harmonic, but here it's played as an artificial—with the right-hand touch point at the 12th fret of the 6th string. For more information on how to play both natural and artificial harmonics, look at the text for Ex. 5.1 (page 55).

On the CD I play Ex. 1.1 first with the pick at a metronome speed of 88 BPM. Then I put the pick down and play it fingerstyle, a little slower, at 70. This example is good for stretching from the left-hand 3rd finger to the 4th, or the 4th finger to the 2nd.

Where "Easy Fifths Exercise 1" expressed its main idea in the space of one measure, the pattern in "Easy Fifths Exercise 2" (**Ex. 1.2;** Tracks 4–5) runs for two bars at a time. The first eight bars are basically the same two-bar phrase, played first in *E,* then *D,* then *G,* and finally *F.* The next eight bars are similar to the first eight, but the second bar of each phrase switches to quarter-notes.

Ex. 1.2   **Easy Fifths Exercise 2**

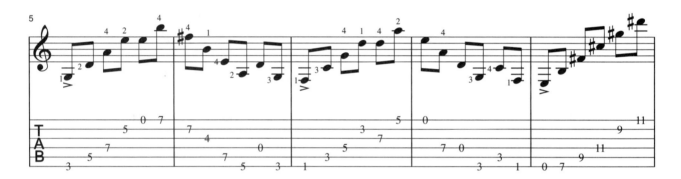

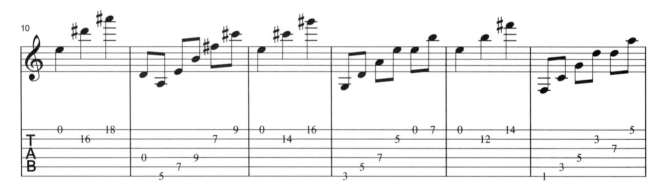

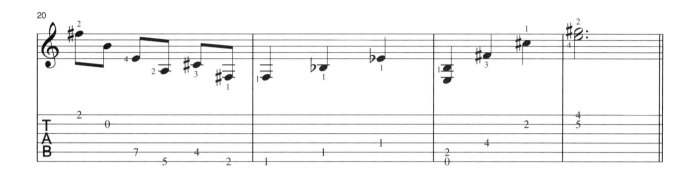

In measures 17–20 the fifths arpeggio is played from the top down rather than the bottom up. Each one-bar phrase goes down in minor thirds, with one little variation: the last notes of measures 18 and 19 go up a fourth rather than down a fifth. Measure 21 is in fourths, ascending, in quarter-notes, and 22 ends the exercise like the previous one with some two-note chords—but no harmonics. On the CD Ex. 1.2 is played first with the pick at 88, then fingerstyle at 80.

FOURTHS EXERCISES
IN MAJOR AND MINOR THIRDS

Now let's look at two more short exercises. The aim of "Fourths Exercise in Major Thirds" (**Ex. 1.3;** Track 6) is to take fourths arpeggios from the bottom up (measures 1–2) or the top down (measures 3–4) and move in two-whole-step, or major-third, jumps.

We have some varied fingering. For example, the fourth measure has the left hand barring strings 3, 4, and 5 at the 3rd fret. Then the (left hand) fingers 4, 3, and 2 line up in a row on the 4th fret to play the arpeggio on strings 4, 5, and 6. I seem to be more successful with this particular combination fingering, but feel free to experiment with either barring or lining up three fingers

Ex. 1.3

Fourths Exercise in Major Thirds

on the same fret to see which technique gives you the best results.

Ex. 1.4 (Track 7), "Fourths Exercise in Minor Thirds," is very much like Ex. 1.3, only this time the shifts are in minor thirds (three half-steps, or one whole-step plus a half). Note that the minor thirds, being smaller, make the eighth-note part of the exercise a bit longer than when we were playing major thirds. As in the previous exercise, there are fingering options here; my choice for the start of the second measure is 2–3–4, first at the 7th fret and then at the 10th. This pattern is mirrored in the second and third beats of the fourth

Ex. 1.4　　　　　　　　　　**Fourths Exercise in Minor Thirds**

bar: 4–3–2, twice, shifting down a minor third. You can just as easily barre these passages—use whatever sounds cleanest.

CHAPTER 2

COMPARING SCALES

So far we've worked with intervals in a linear, arpeggiated way, plus we've used different intervals (minor third, major third, whole-step) to move these lines around. Now let's look at some exercises from non-jazz sources and delve further into how intervals shape lines and chords.

SWINGIN' WITH SLONIMSKY

A book that jazz musicians have consulted over the years is *Thesaurus of Scales and Melodic Patterns,* by Nicolas Slonimsky. It is based on the nearly 480 million possible combinations of the 12-tone chromatic scale. This is considered a classical book, so there are no phrases defined as "jazz," yet there's an excerpt in the introduction of a cycle of fourths (*A♭* to *D♯* to *F♯* to *B,* etc.) using single-note lines comprising dominant 7♭9 scales—an idea familiar to jazz players. There are many ideas in 20th-century classical music that have been used in jazz. For example, I discovered in Slonimsky the source of one of my favorite scales, the 1-plus-2 (or 2-plus-1) diminished scale; it's attributed to Rimsky-Korsakov.

If we choose some of Slonimsky's single-note examples and put chords to them, we get scales that apply to jazz. Here are some examples.

Ex. 2.1

Slonimsky Ex. 1

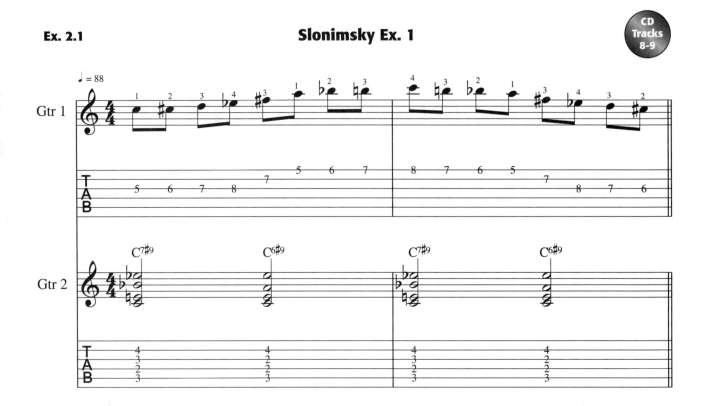

Ex. 2.1, "Slonimsky Ex. 1" (Tracks 8–9), is a *C* diminished arpeggio (upward from *C, E♭–F♯–A–C*) with two half-steps between the *C* and *E♭* and two half-steps between the *A* and *C*. Putting chords to this scale is kind of arbitrary, but in addition to the obvious connection to a *C* diminished chord, I think a *C7♯9* fits this scale quite well, because of the *E♭* common to both chords. To correspond better with the last four notes of each measure, one note (*B♭*) of the *C7♯9* is changed to *A,* and the chord becomes *C6♯9*.

For **Ex. 2.2,** "Slonimsky Ex. 2" (Tracks 10–11), I found a scale with four whole-steps in it: *C–C♯–D,* then *E–F♯–G♯–B♭,* followed by *B♮.* Because of the whole-steps, dominant 7♯5 chords (related to augmented chords) in *F♯, G♯, B♭,* and *C* are appropriate matches for this scale, except for the last note, *C♯,* for which I changed to an *A7♯5* chord.

Ex. 2.2   **Slonimsky Ex. 2**

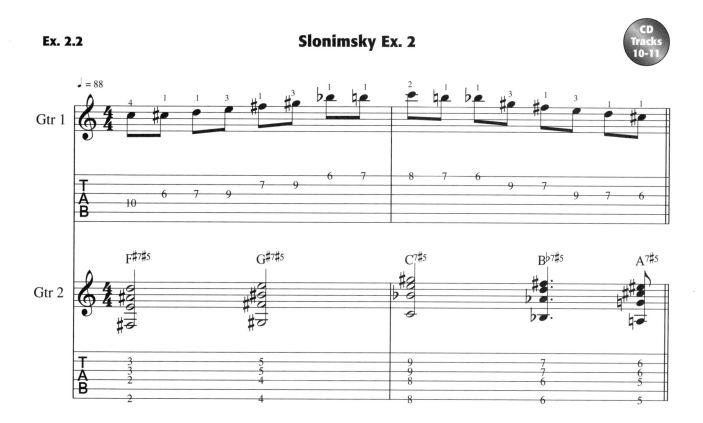

The next scale is presented in two formats: "Slonimsky Ex. 3A" and "Slonimsky Ex. 3B," Examples 2.3 and 2.4. **Ex. 2.3** (Tracks 12–13)**,** like the two previous examples, has one guitar playing the scale and a second guitar playing the chords. This scale goes, upward from *C*, whole-step, half-step, whole-step, half-step (2-plus-1, twice), then half-step, whole-step, half-step (1-plus-2 plus 1). You will see in the next section that this scale sounds close to the Rimsky-Korsakov. This scale can be harmonized with two raised 9 chords a half-step apart, namely, *B7#9* and *C7#9*. I changed the first *B7#9* to a *B7♭9* to match the first note of the scale, *C*.

Ex. 2.4, "Slonimsky Ex. 3B" (Track 14), is for one guitar, reworking the 3A scale into one line of single notes and chords. There are twice as many chords in this example, but they still follow the same progression as 3A. What we have

Ex. 2.3

Slonimsky Ex. 3A

here are different *voicings* (rearrangements of, or additions to, the notes of the same chord), like the chord on the third beat of the first bar. It looks like an *F#13,* but in this sequence it's a *C7#9#11* without the *C* bass being played. The next chord (fourth beat) is the same voicing up a minor third. Again, like the previous chord, it looks like it could be an *A13,* but here it is an *Eb7#9#11* without the *Eb* bass note.

The pattern of a chord followed by a single note in bar 1 is reversed in bar 2—single note, chord, single note, chord, etc. Because the chords' top notes are different, the voicings become 7#9s. Also, the first two, *Eb7#9* and *C7#9,* have the third on the bottom (*G* and *E*), while the last two, *D7#9* and *B7#9,* have the root on the bottom.

For examples that include two guitar parts, on the CD I play both parts of

Ex. 2.4   **Slonimsky Ex. 3B**

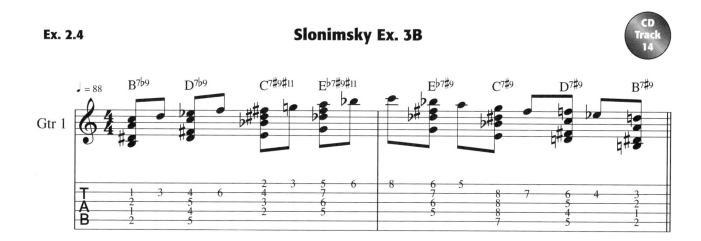

each example first, then I play Guitar 2 in order for you to play Guitar 1. This way you can stop and check the voicings or the differences between one scale and another. Finally, on the CD I ran Guitar 2 of Examples 2.1, 2.2, and 2.3 (Tracks 15–16) without any breaks so you can play Guitar 1 straight through.

SCALE SIMILARITIES

We are almost ready to use these ideas in a real musical situation, but let's do one more preparation. Let's change key, to *F*, and look at five scales, all quite similar, plus I'll introduce a variation on the fifth scale. The aim is to see how all these scales can figure in the composition and improvisation of a 12-bar blues.

In **Ex. 2.5** (Tracks 17–28) we have several similar scales: the "Slonimsky Ex. 3" scale (Examples 2.3 and 2.4), *G♭* jazz minor (superlocrian mode, which starts from *F*), 1-plus-2, whole-tone, whole-tone/chromatic, and a variation on the whole-tone/chromatic.

Compare the Slonimsky scale to the jazz minor; both scales include parts of a diminished arpeggio—*F, A♭,* and *B♮.* "Slonimsky Ex. 3" also has a *D,* continuing the diminished arpeggio, but jazz minor has no *D.* They both have *E♭*s before the octave *F*s.

Ex. 2.5   **Scale Similarities**

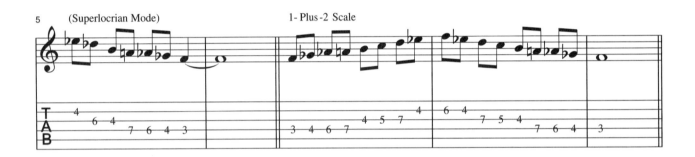

Next, compare the jazz minor scale with the 1-plus-2 scale. The intervals of the first five notes are half-step (1), whole-step (2), half-step (1), whole-step (2), the same for both scales. After the fifth note in the jazz minor, the last three notes go up in whole-steps. This whole-step section of the scale makes it work well for ♯11 and ♯5 chords. After the fifth note in the 1-plus-2, the scale remains symmetrical; that is, the same sequence of intervals continues: 1-plus-2, twice.

Now play the whole-tone scale, which, in this instance, goes from *F* all the way up to *A* above the octave and back down. These are all whole-steps (2) as opposed to half-steps (1). This scale can sound good in any augmented or 7♯5 chord with a bass note of *F, G, A, B, D♭,* or *E♭* (like the 7♯5 chords in "Slonimsky Ex. 2"). This scale also sounds good with two-note chords built with major thirds, as we will see in the improvisation section on the blues.

The whole-tone/chromatic scale is just like the whole-tone scale except we add half-steps between the *F* and the *G*, the *G* and the *A*, the *B* and the *C♯*, and the *C♯* and the *E♭*. This scale contains ten notes in one octave—just two notes shy of being a chromatic scale.

The 3/4 variation of the whole-tone/chromatic scale takes the last five descending notes (bar 15) and adds the *E♭* below the *F* (bar 16). That phrase is played up a minor third (bar 17), then again up a minor third (bar 18).

These examples show us that changing a few notes to create a different but similar scale can make a subtle but meaningful difference in a line. Altering the scale also affects the harmony related to that line, giving us ideas that break away from the standard modes (Ionian, Dorian, Phrygian, etc.). The use of chromatic passages in these scales gives a freer, less predictable quality to both written and improvised lines, as you will see in the next chapter.

CHAPTER 3

BLUES SOLOING

Let's take a look at how some of the scale ideas in Ex. 2.5 can work in a piece of music. In **Ex. 3.1** (Tracks 29–30), the melody of "Blues for Yoshihiro Hattori," the whole-tone/chromatic variation is used to create a more abstract sound on the *F7* chord, and this same variation shows up again in the improvisation as part of a longer idea.

This melody takes up two choruses of blues (six bars of 12/8 are equivalent to 12 bars of 4/4). The second melody chorus is almost entirely different from the first. Bar 5 in the first chorus is basically the same as bar 11 in the second, except that in the first chorus, the guitar plays beats 10–12 a minor third above the saxophone.

The chords underneath the melody are not normal blues changes. Some of these are *slash* chords, like *F#maj6/9/G;* others are *altered* chords (any extension of dominant seventh), like *A13♭9* or *B7#9*. The chords have their own sense of movement, and they complement the melody by going against it. Because of this contrary harmony–melody relationship, don't expect the melody scales to always correspond to the chords' scales. The dissonances between the chords and melody don't last for long because both are moving, sometimes going their separate ways and creating dissonance (as in measure 2) or coming together and becoming less dissonant (as in measure 3).

Ex. 3.1

Melody of "Blues for Yoshihiro Hattori"

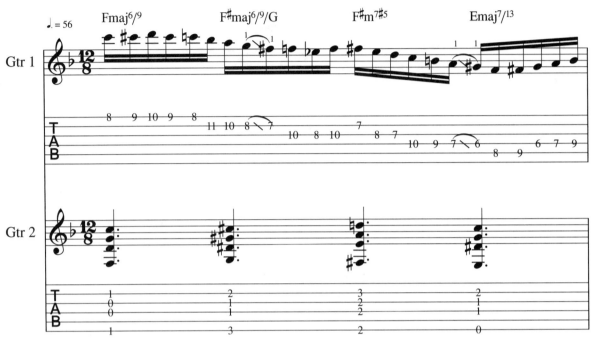

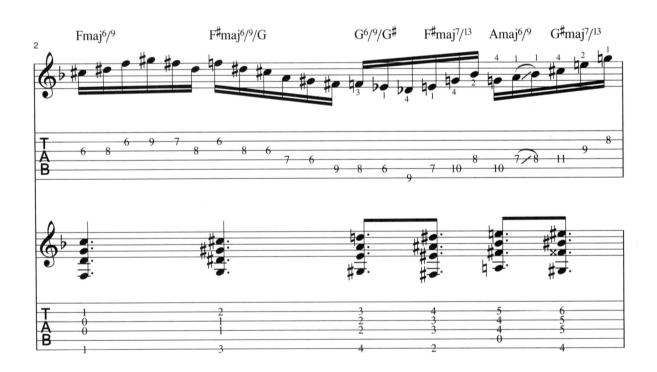

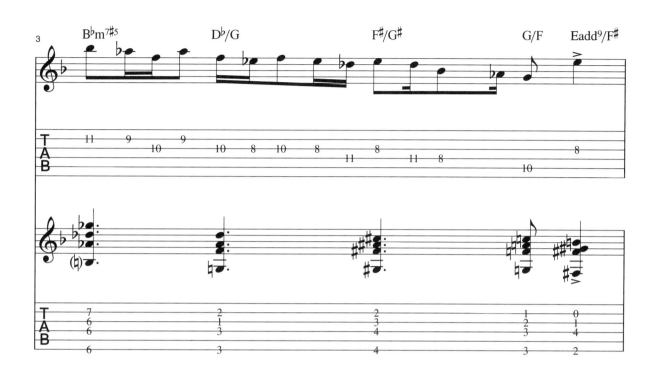

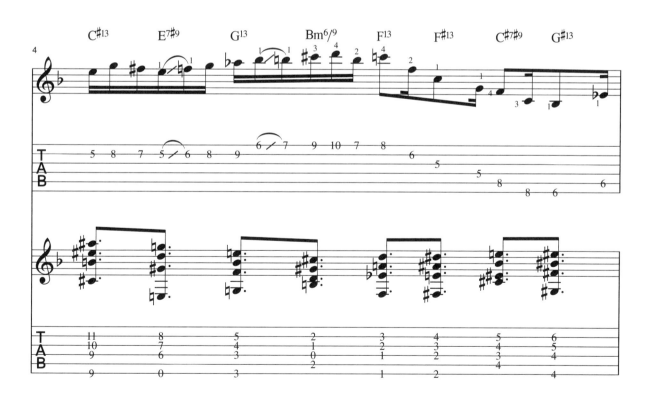

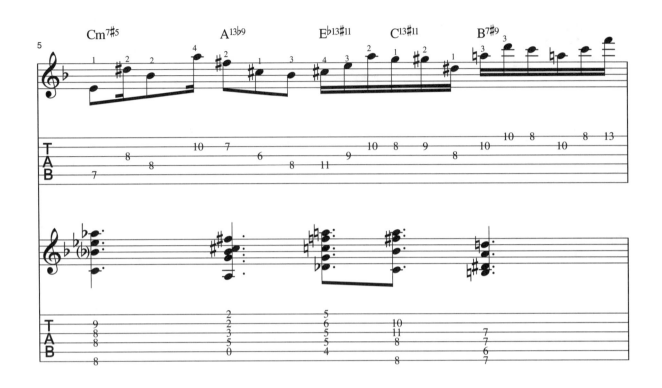

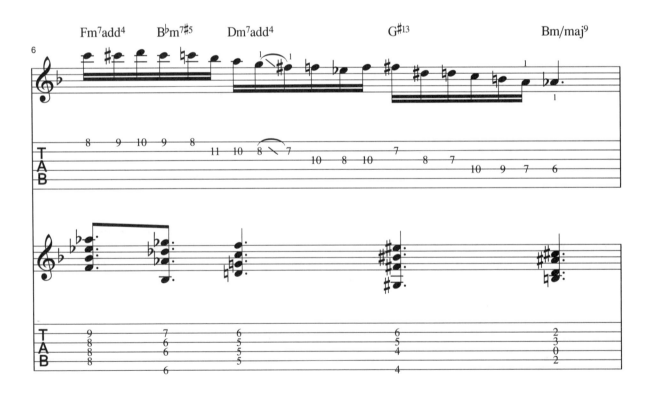

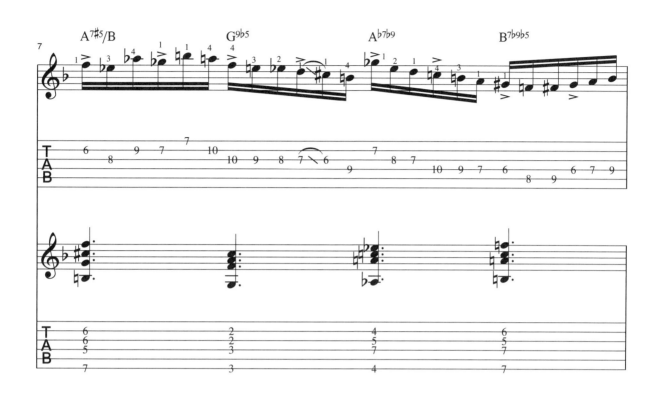

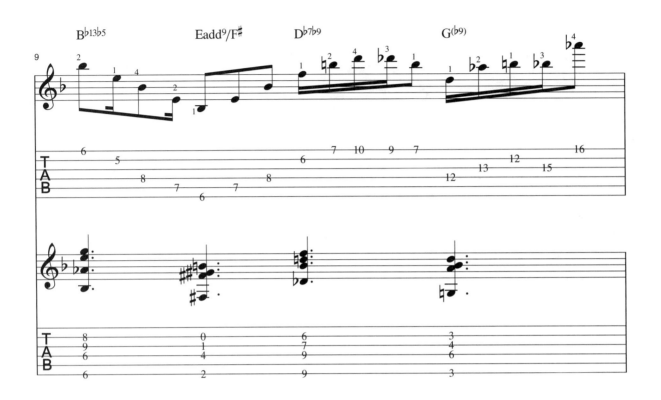

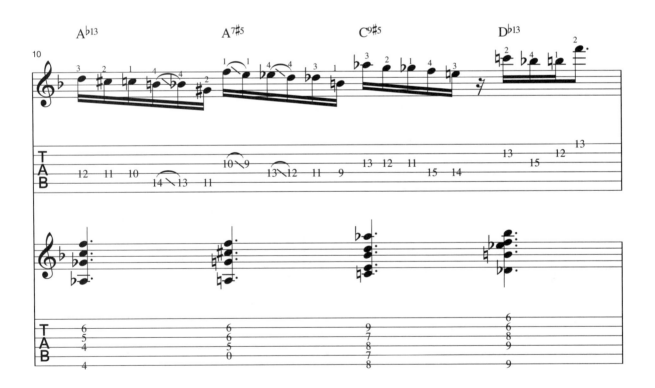

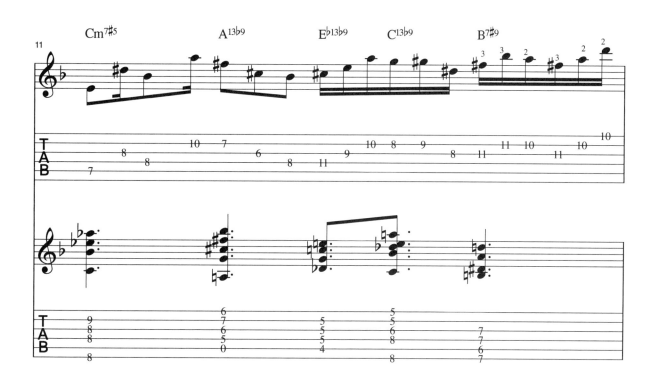

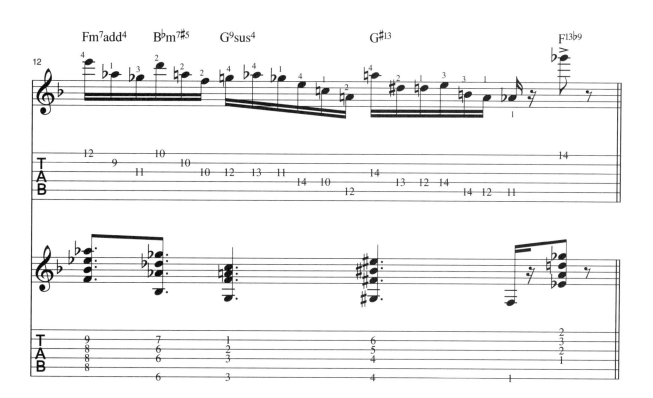

FITTING SCALES WITH MELODY

Ex. 3.2 shows how the various scales from Ex. 2.5 appear in the melody of "Blues for Yoshihiro Hattori." The Rimsky-Korsakov diminished (1-plus-2 or 2-plus-1) scale is used a lot. The *F#* jazz minor scale (which is the same as the *Gb* jazz minor in Ex. 2.5) is also out in full force, and the *A* jazz minor shows up in the last measure (bar 12). The whole-tone scale is used in the first three beats of bar 9 and in the last three beats of bar 10. Also, as promised earlier, the whole-tone/chromatic variation appears in the first nine beats of measure 10. There are also uses of the Dorian and Mixolydian modes, including a variation, Dorian b5, in bar 12.

   Ex. 3.3 (Tracks 31–35) shows the full scales that are used in this melody. Note that in some scales I play additional notes that are out of the scale, called *passing tones*. These notes are not notated with the scales, but I talk about them on the CD and play the scale first without the passing tones, and then with them, so you can hear the difference. In the first half of measure 4 of the melody (Ex. 3.2), there's an *F#* passing tone in a 1-plus-2 scale from *E*. In beats 7–9 of bar 5, there is a *G#* passing tone inside the 2-plus-1 scale from *C#*. In beats 10–12 of measure 10, there are two passing tones in the *G* whole-tone scale: *Bb* and *C*. Finally, in beats 7–9 of measure 11, the *F#* 2-plus-1 scale has a *Bb* passing tone.

Ex. 3.2   **"Blues for Yoshihiro Hattori" – Melody Scales**

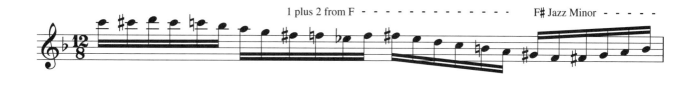

Ex. 3.3   **"Blues for Yoshihiro Hattori" – Full Scales**

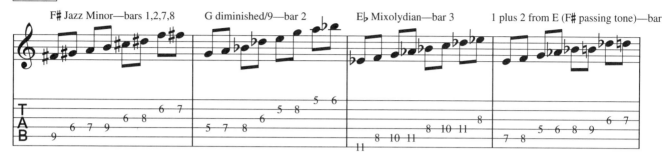

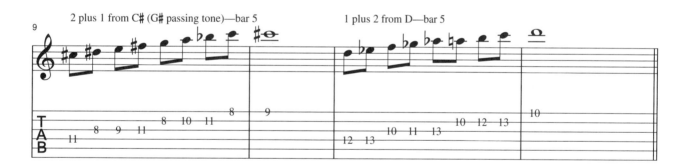

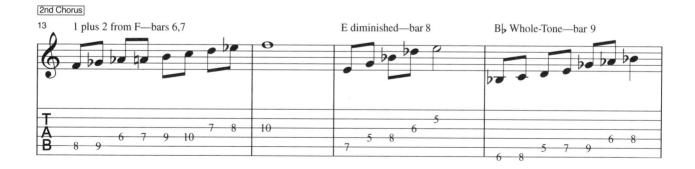

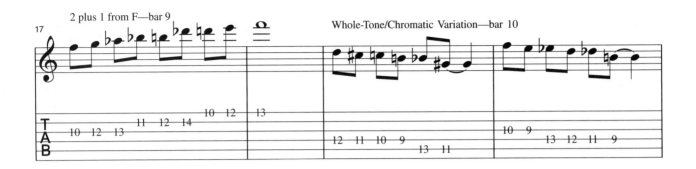

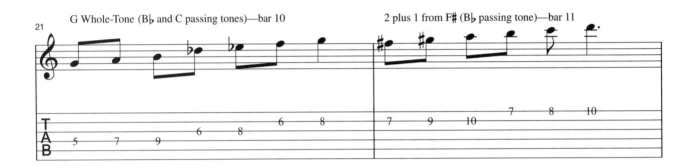

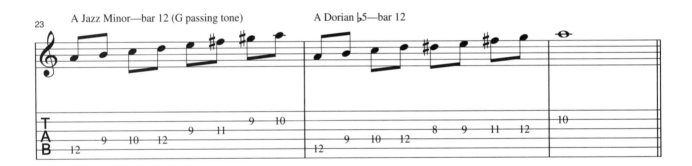

IMPROVISING WITH SCALES

Now that you've learned the melody of "Blues for Yoshihiro Hattori," let's look at how the interval shapes in the line can be used again in the improvisation. Sometimes the improvised ideas are close to the melody, and sometimes they are further away. Also, the melody intervals and the movement of the chords have the tendency to encourage chromatic passages in the improvisation. Let's see how all this happens in two choruses of improv.

A lot of the ideas in this solo transcription (**Ex. 3.4;** Tracks 36–38) come from the scales used in the melody. These are: symmetrical diminished scales, like 1-plus-2 or 2-plus-1, the jazz minor (especially the whole-tone part, which can lead to augmented arpeggios), plus the scale derived from the Slonimsky examples, the whole-tone/chromatic variation.

I worked with an *Eb* augmented arpeggio in the first two measures of the first chorus because the sound of the whole-tone/augmented mode implies an *F7#11*. Then for measure 3 (normally the IV7 chord—*Bb7*) I started to play a *D* augmented (the last two notes of bar 2 are *Eb* and *G*, then the first two notes of bar 3 are down a half step, *D* and *F#*). That in turn developed into a *D* whole-tone scale starting on the second half of beat 5 in measure 3.

The whole-tone/chromatic variation shows up in bar 4 (the return to the tonic in a normal progression) starting on the *F* on the last 16th of beat 3, going down chromatically to *C#*, then dropping a whole-step to *B*. The idea continues with a 1-plus-2 from *G* continuing up to *D*, then going up a minor third to end on *F* and *Gb*.

Measure 5, which in a regularly harmonized blues would be the *C7*, or V7, chord, starts with a tumbling chromatic line and ends with phrases from the *F* whole-tone scale.

Measure 6, the return to the tonic plus the turnaround section in a normal blues, has a bit of chromatic jabbing at a familiar blues phrase and ends with a blues-based double-stops idea.

We start the second chorus, measure 7, with *F* whole-tone/augmented double-stops. Then the solo goes into a displaced chromatic scale with variations; that is, I'm thinking, Play a chromatic scale but alter the register (octave) with each note, as well as, Don't play it verbatim—mix it up a bit with some minor thirds and tritones.

The double-stops continue in measure 8, and then starting on beat 9 of measure 8 we have tritones: *B♮* to *F,* then *A♮* to two *E♭s.* From the second *E♭,* the line goes down a fourth to *B♭* (8th fret, 4th string), which in turn jumps down a minor ninth to *A* (5th fret, 6th string). Then we go up a major seventh to *G♯* (6th fret, 4th string). This type of fractured chromatic phrasing goes on to beat 9 of bar 10, where there's an upward chromatic passage leading into measure 11. Measure 11 uses a *D♯* 1-plus-2 scale for the chord changes that would normally have the V7 chord. The last three notes, *G♭* up a major seventh to *F* and down a fourth to *C,* set us up for the interval pattern in the last bar.

This final bar has interval shapes in 16th-notes of major third, fourth, and fourth (beats 1–3), then tritone, fourth, and fourth (beats 4–6). From this point, starting from beat 7, the thinking is now "normal" blues pentatonic; the last phrase, a blues cliché, sets up a call-and-response exchange with the saxophone for the next chorus, which returns to a normal blues.

Ex. 3.4   **Solo Transcription of "Blues for Yoshihiro Hattori"**

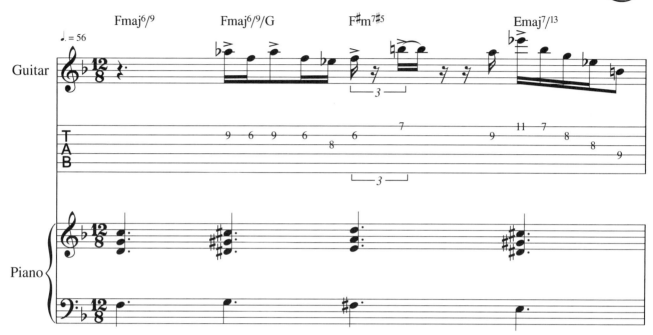

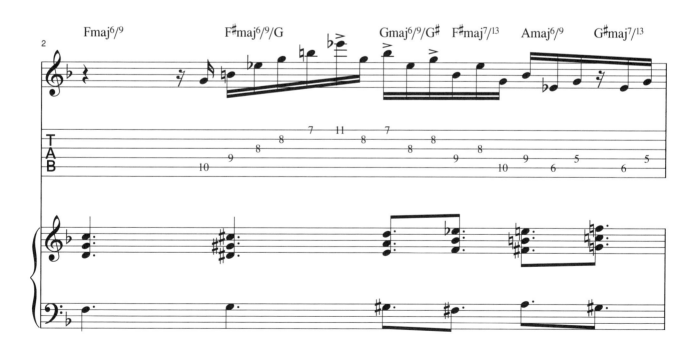

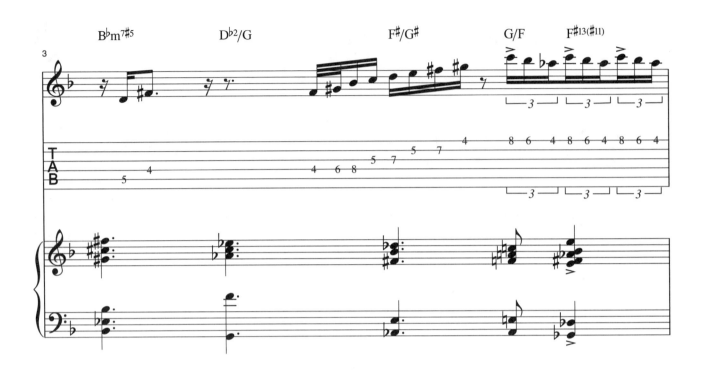

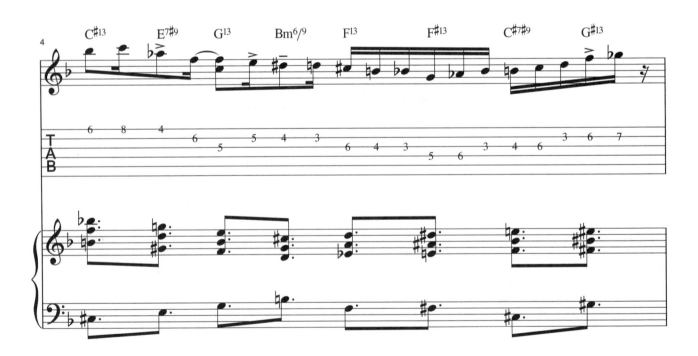

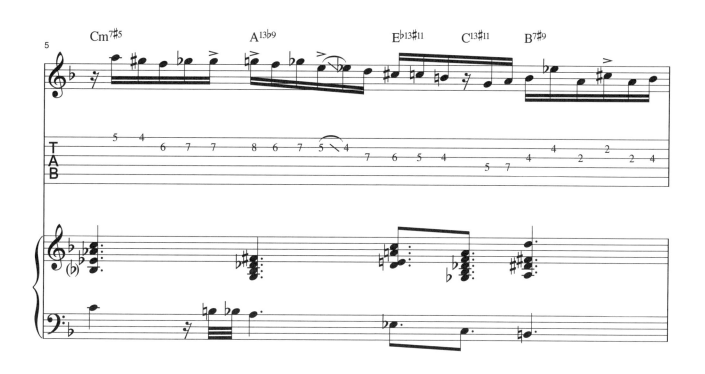

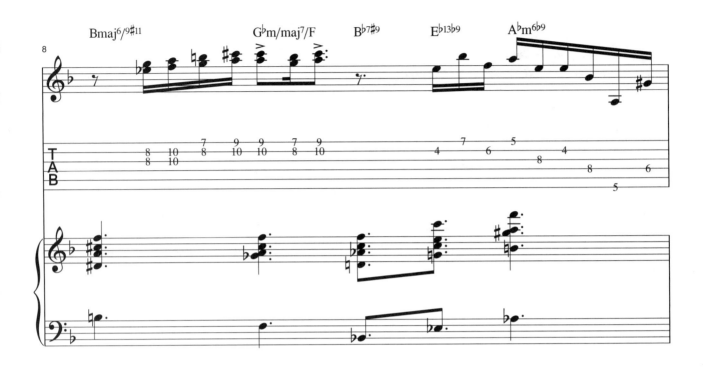

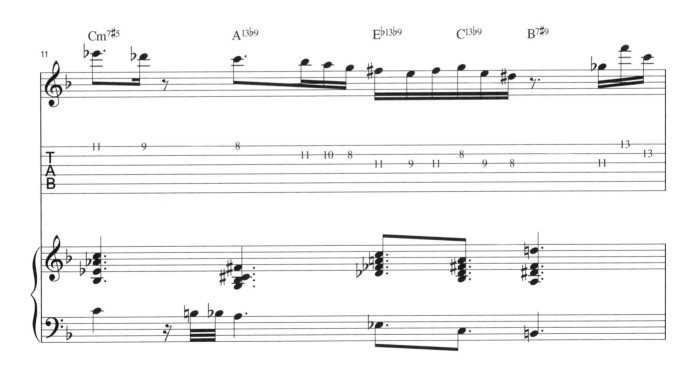

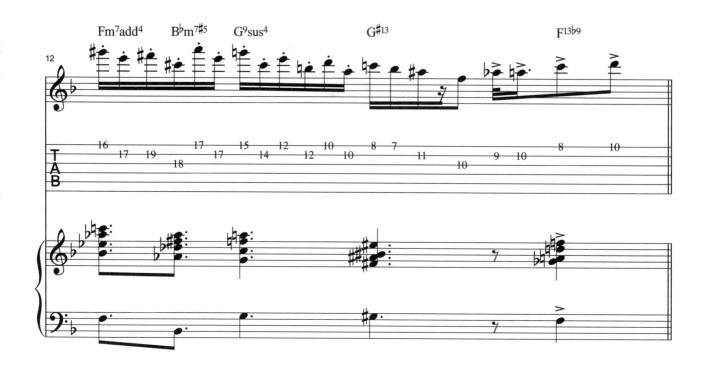

PLAYING OVER ALTERED CHORDS

We have now completed an examination of intervals, both horizontally and vertically, as well as some different scales and their application in improvising. Along the way we've seen how the melody and chords of any given piece influence the kind of scales or intervals you use in your improvisation. Before we leave these ideas about how intervals shape lines and chords, and how lines and chords shape the improvisation, I want to go back and play on some altered chords so you can hear them and respond accordingly.

In soloing it's not just *what* scale is used but also *how* and *how much* it is used. The examples in this section vary in how much each scale is used, both note-wise and rhythmically. On the CD I've transcribed passages from real playing scenarios. First I play the transcribed segment over Guitar 2, then I run the same passage again for you to play.

In **Ex. 3.5** (Tracks 39–40), the *A* jazz minor scale corresponds to the *F#m7b5/9* (altered m7b5) chord, but you can also view *F#m7b5/9* as an *E* augmented triad (*E, G#, C*) suspended over *F#,* or a *C* augmented triad (*C, E, G#*) over *A* (with the *F#* silent).

In this example, the solo comes in on beat 2 of the second measure with the *C* augmented triad idea. It stays in the *A* jazz minor scale by going to *B♮* in the next bar, not *C*. The solo uses more of a straight-eighth-note feel, responding to the accompaniment (also known as *comping*), which has strong but not obvious accents. The comper doesn't have to add the ninth to the *F#m7b5:* the soloist does it.

Ex. 3.5   **altered m7♭5**

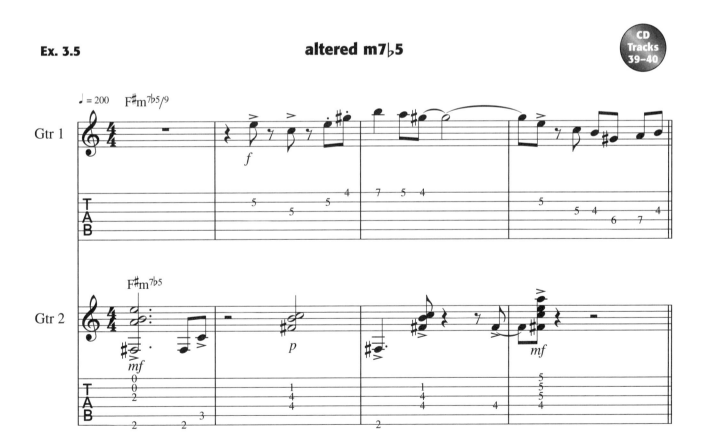

Ex. 3.6 (Tracks 41–42) is a IIm7♭5–V7♯5–I progression in *C* minor, where, in the first bar, the soloist uses a *C* harmonic minor scale (*C–D–E♭–F–G–A♭–B♮–C*) to negotiate the *Dm7♭5* to *G7♯5*. In bars 2 (*C* minor) and 3 (*A♭7♯11*), five notes of *E♭* jazz minor are used: the last two notes of the second bar (*C♮* and *D♮*) and the first three notes (*E♭, F,* and *G♭*) of bar 3. Into the third bar the scale becomes *E♭* Dorian because the *D* is replaced by *D♭*.

Ex. 3.7 (Tracks 43–44) is a six-bar passage in 3/4 time. *Bm7♭5* to *E7* (♭9 or ♯9) comes up twice. Look at the chromatic eighth-note passage in the first two bars—the first note of bar 1 and the first note of bar 2 form a tritone (*B* to *F*) interval, which is also the interval basic to *Bm7♭5*. The entire second bar and the first two notes of the third bar are an *F* jazz minor scale. When it goes to *Bm7♭5* the second time, the improv plays a simple idea, *F–E–G–F–E*. This is still *F* jazz minor, but only three notes of the scale are used.

Ex. 3.8 (Tracks 45–46) is similar to Ex. 3.7, but this passage is four bars long instead of three. The lead-in is the *A♭* jazz minor arpeggio in the first bar, anticipating the second bar, where the solo plays a bop phrase using *C* harmonic minor. The *E♭* jazz minor scale starts in bar 3, where the *G♭* in the scale turns the *Cm9* into *Cm9♭5*. Bar 4 (*A♭13♯11*) is all *E♭* jazz minor. Another way to define this scale is *A♭* Lydian ♭7. Look at the run from *A♭* (second 16th-note of beat 2 in bar 4) up to the next *A♭*—it's a Lydian scale, with the ♭7 (*G♭*) instead of the major 7 (*G♮*).

Ex. 3.6

m7♭5 to 7♯5 to m7 to 7♯11

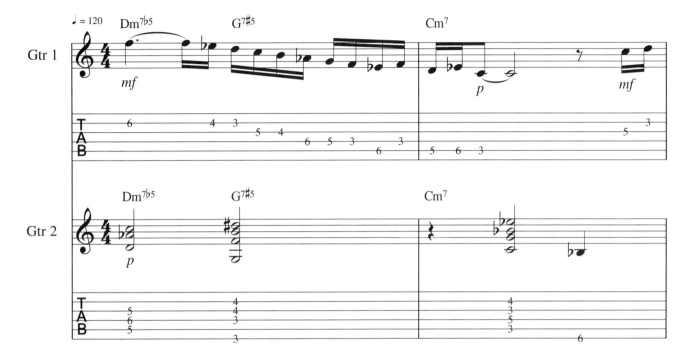

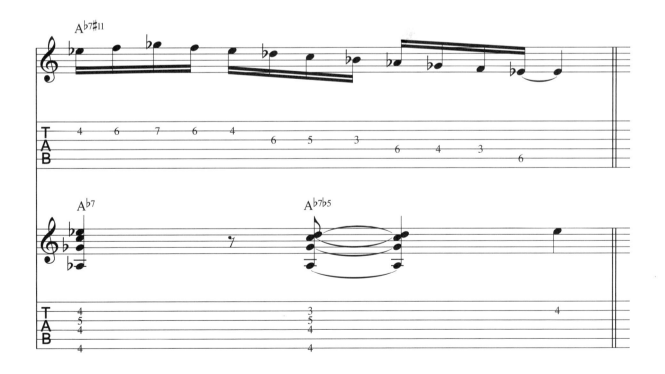

Ex. 3.7

m7♭5 to m7♭5

Ex. 3.8 **m7♭5 to 7♭9 to m9 to 7♯11 with lead-in**

CHAPTER 4

CREATIVE COMPING

Now let's explore an area with which we ended the book *Jazz Guitar*—playing with a rhythm section.

THE IN AND THE OUT

We'll set up a standard chord-change bass line, comp over that line in a more traditional, literal style, then do the same section playing in a more abstract or "out" style.

The chord sequence is five bars: one bar apiece of *C7, F7, Em7b5, A7b9,* and *Dm7*. The literal comping version, **Ex. 4.1** (Track 47), sticks to the score closely, anticipating and substituting a little bit, like in the last half of beat 4 of measure 1, where the comp pushes (or anticipates) the *F7* that comes in the next measure. Then the comp substitutes a *Bb9* (the *Bb* bass note is implied) on the last eighth-note of measure 2 for the *Em7b5* that will come in measure 3. Again we get a push of the *A7b9* on the last eighth-note of measure 3.

Ex. 4.2 (Track 48), the "out" version, starts by contrast with accented eighth-notes using the *E* up to *D#* major-seventh interval; that makes the *C7* a *C7#9*. Then on the third beat of measure 1 the comp reverses the initial phrase (*D#* down to *E*), down an octave. In the next measure the comp picks a dominant-seventh interval out of an *F9* chord, *A* up to *G*. The comp then rests until the third beat of measure 3, where it plays a major seventh going *Ab* up to *G* (that implies a *Bb13*). This is followed an eighth-rest later by two notes from an *A7#9*, *C#* on the 3rd string and a *C♮* on the 1st string, which pushes into the next measure (*A7b9*). In measure 4 comes another two-note chord (the interval of a second—*C#* and *D#*); this adds a *b5* to the *A7*. Finally there's a three-eighth-note hit with a two-note chord (*G* and *Ab*) in the fifth, or *Dm7*, measure, which implies (for that measure) a *Dm7b5* and also anticipates the *b9* of the *G7* chord that would follow if we continued the progression.

Now look at **Ex. 4.3** (Track 49), a literal solo idea straight out of a swing-bop vocabulary. Note that the major-seventh upward arpeggio in measure 3 of the progression leads to augmented usage in the next bar. This is pretty much playing each chord as it stands with no outlandish substitutions.

By contrast, **Ex. 4.4** (Track 50), the "out" solo idea, starts with a four-note phrase out of the harmony (*B–C#–E–F#*). Interval-wise, it's I–II–IV–V in eighth-notes, and each new phrase goes down in whole-steps until we reach the third bar of the progression. That four-note pattern starts out like it wants to keep repeating, but it mutates into a fragment of *D* harmonic minor in the fourth bar. Then, in the third beat, it goes to a fourths arpeggio: *C#–F#–B*. The next *B*, down one octave, starts another arpeggio of fourths, crossing into the fifth bar. At that point the line stays with eccentric interval shapes, like *C* (beat 2, bar 5), down a fourth to *G*, down a tritone to *C#*, and up a ninth to *D#*. The aim of the line here is to avoid the obvious harmony and keep jumping around.

Ex. 4.1

Literal Comping Idea

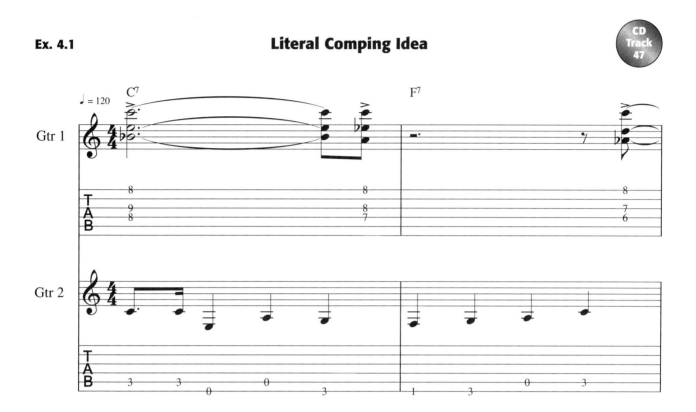

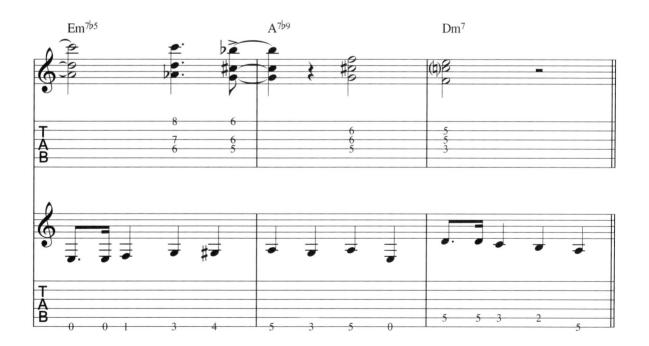

Ex. 4.2

"Out" Comping Idea

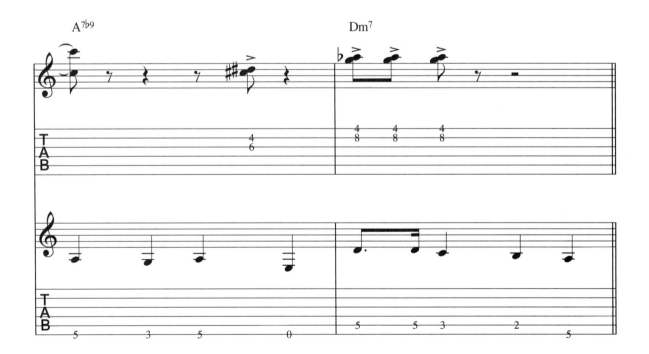

Ex. 4.3

Literal Solo Idea

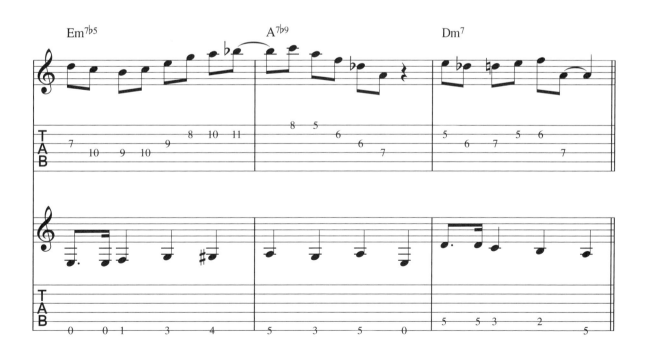

Ex. 4.4   **"Out" Solo Idea**

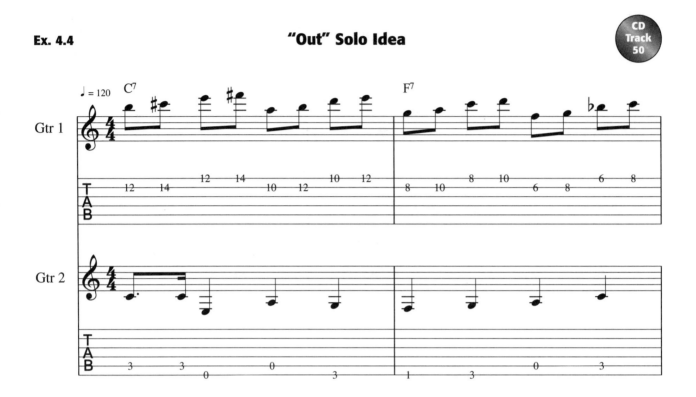

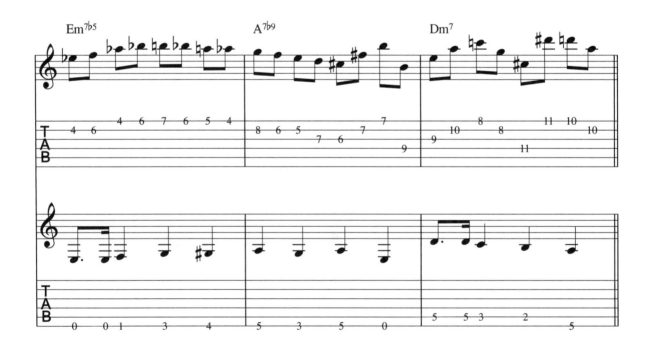

COMPING ALONE

When you don't have piano or another guitar in your ensemble, you don't encounter any chord-clashing situations. You have more freedom, but with that freedom comes a responsibility to clarify and guide the harmony.

In **Ex. 4.5** (Tracks 51–53), an excerpt from the adagio section of the composition "Pedals and Suspensions," there is a 15-bar melody using familiar chords: maj7, 13, 7♭5, m7♭5, 7♭9, and so forth. The bass doubles *some* of the low passing tones of the guitar in measures 5–7 and in measure 11. The guitar is doubling the melody with the soprano saxophone, and the top note of each guitar chord is also a melody note. Normally I suggest the guitar not play the melody when there's a horn already doing it, but in this case the aim is to create an ensemble sound with two melody voices plus chords.

Remember the chord forms you know already, like, in measures 1 and 12, the *Cmaj7/9/E* (also known as an *Em7♯5*). File that chord away for the next time you have to play a *C* major chord melody with the fifth on top. The same thing applies to all the other chords here: Know that the next time you have a minor chord with the melody on the fifth degree, the *Em9* inversion in measure 4 will work. Or, when you encounter a melody with the ♭5, remember that the *A7♭5* in bar 4 is one available inversion.

Measure 5 is a bit different animal in that the guitar hits the *Fmaj7* inversion with the major third (the melody note) on top, then goes down the *F* major scale with the bass and catches the melody note (*G*) on the fourth beat. File away that *Fmaj7* inversion as one choice you'll have when that melody/chord situation presents itself again.

On the CD, the excerpt from the group recording is played first (Track 51); then I do another pass, playing just the guitar part (Track 53).

Ex. 4.5

Excerpt from "Pedals"

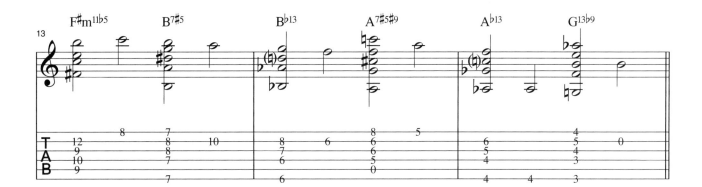

HARMONIZING WITH A
PRIMARY CHORD PROGRESSION

When you are working with another instrument that plays chords, it's important that everyone knows what the basic changes are. Then you need to be able to add, if needed, to the primary chords, or to reinforce an important interval where it's appropriate.

In **Ex. 4.6** (Tracks 54–56)**,** the progression starts with three bars of *Dmaj7/9* and goes to a *Gmaj7* for one bar, then to four bars of a *D7* altered chord. Note that the primary chords are played by Guitar 2, which has its 6th string tuned down to *D.* The top guitar (Guitar 1) is tuned normally.

In bar 1, Guitar 1 supports the *Dmaj7/9* with a 1–3–5–maj7 (*Amaj7*) chord, and in bar 2 that chord is changed (3, or *C♯,* down to *B*) to *Amaj7/9*. In bar 3 we have, from the bottom up, *B–E–A–C♯,* which I'm calling *Bsus* (*A* triad over *B* bass), but this is also the upper structure of *Dmaj7/6/9.* Similarly, in the next measure, Guitar 1's *Bm7♯5* becomes a *Gmaj7* if you put a *G* on the bottom. It's still basically three bars of *Dmaj7,* then one bar of *Gmaj7.*

Now we get to the four bars of the altered *D7* chord, where Guitar 2 plays *D9♯11* for two measures and *D13♯11* for two. Guitar 1's chords are spelled: *Cmaj7♯5, Cmaj9♯5,* and *D9♭5,* and then there are two quarter-note voicings in the last bar, *Eadd4* to *Asus2*. They support the primary chords and, like the primary chords, these upper chords contain only notes from the *A* jazz minor scale.

By the way, in terms of improvising over the *D9#11* and *D13#11*, don't think you have to play the entire *A* jazz minor scale. You can simply play, for example, an *Amaj7* interval (*A–G#*) or a *Cmaj7* interval (*C–B*) while letting the chords underneath do the work.

Ex. 4.6   **Harmonizing with a Primary Chord Progression**

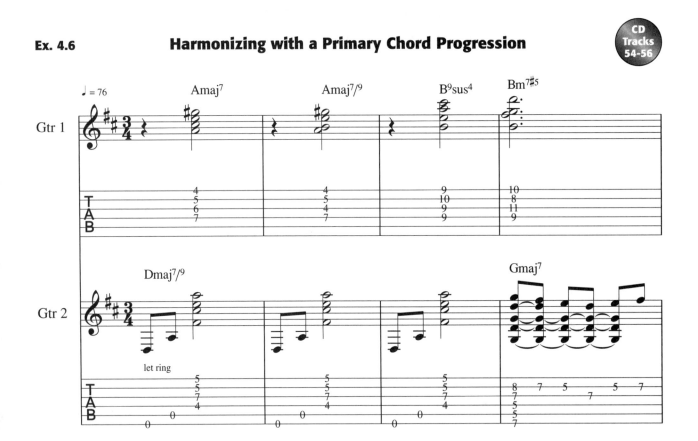

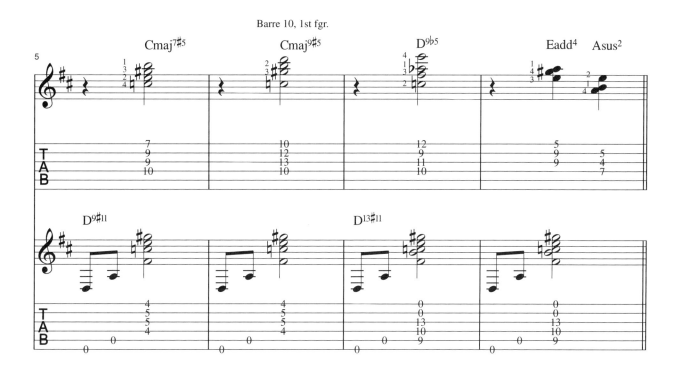

CHAPTER 5

EXPLORING
NEW TECHNIQUES

Now let's move to several ways to expand your technique—starting with natural and artificial harmonics. The composition we will look at first was introduced in the book *Jazz Guitar,* and we've updated it from "Turkish Coffee" to "Turkish Coffee 2000" for purposes of differentiation. I have since recorded the piece, so it's been expanded to include an intro and several blowing choruses, some of which are transcribed here.

NATURAL AND ARTIFICIAL HARMONICS

We begin **Ex. 5.1** (Track 57)**,** the intro, in measure 1 with a natural harmonic: a *B* played by plucking the 2nd string while touching, not fretting, the 12th fret. While the *B* harmonic continues to ring into the second beat, play some "normal" notes: *C* on the 1st string, *F* on the 3rd string, back to *C.* Then you play another natural harmonic, *D* (4th string, 12th fret), on the second eighth-note of beat 4, and it rings into the second measure. On the fourth beat of the second measure there is another *D* natural harmonic, called a *double harmonic* or *double octave* because it is two octaves above the open string. This high *D,* played by touching the 4th string at the 5th fret, rings into the third measure.

We start using artificial harmonics in measure 4. These are played by

Ex. 5.1

"Turkish Coffee 2000" – Intro

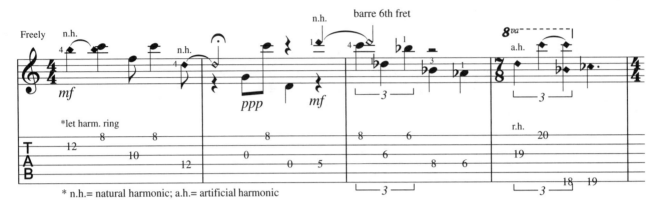

* n.h.= natural harmonic; a.h.= artificial harmonic

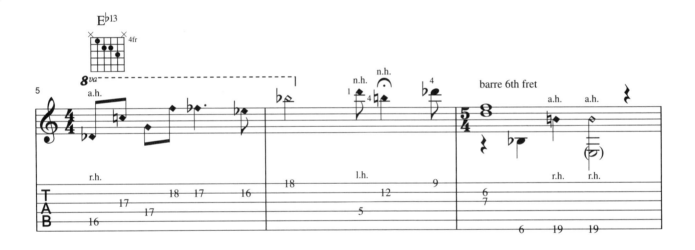

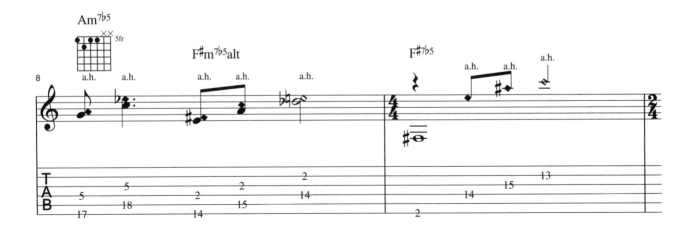

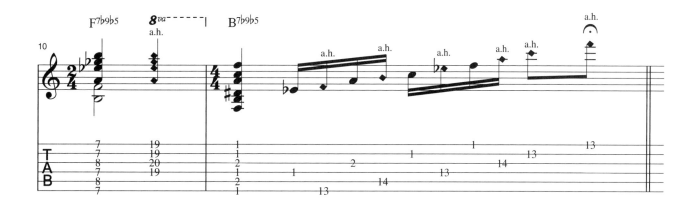

touching the fret points (19th fret of the 3rd string, 20th fret of the 1st string, etc.) with the tip of the 1st (index) finger of the right hand, while the pick, held between the thumb and second finger, plucks the string. The right-hand "fret points" are each 12 frets above where the left hand is fingering, making the notes one octave higher.

In measure 5, look at the chord diagram to see the left-hand position for the first four notes, and watch out in bar 6 for the same *D* double harmonic as in bar 2. The last note of bar 6, a "normal" *D♭*, serves as a pickup to bar 7, which starts with the first finger barring the 6th fret across all the strings to play the *B♭* major chord. Then on the third beat, the left hand lifts up to play an artificial harmonic at the 19th fret, 6th string. On the fourth beat, same fret, lift your right index finger slightly and play the artificial harmonic so it sounds out two notes: the harmonic *B* and the open *E* will sound together.

Beginning in measure 8, we have a series of "normal" notes and artificial harmonics played together, two strings apart. In other words, the first finger of the right hand goes to the harmonic touch point, which in the first instance is the *A* on the 17th fret, 6th string. At the same time, the right-hand pinky plucks the normal *G* at the 5th fret of the 4th string. Since the harmonic makes the

A on the 6th string come up one octave, the *A* and *G* sound as a second interval. This is followed with an *Eb* artificial harmonic (18th fret, 5th string) and a normal *C* (5th fret, 3rd string) sounding as a minor third.

Next is the *F#m7b5* altered starting on the third beat (the time signature is 5/4). It's like the previous arpeggio except there are three combinations of harmonics and normal notes—strings 6 and 4, 5 and 3, and 4 and 2. Measure 9 returns to 4/4. The first note of the *F#7b5* is normal, while the rest are artificial harmonics.

For measure 10, sweeping the tip of the 1st finger of the right hand in one motion across the frets plays the harmonics part of the *F7b9b5*. Getting those notes to ring out may take some practice.

Measure 11 takes the same chord as bar 10 and drops it down a tritone so it becomes *B7b7b5*. The arpeggio here alternates normal notes (*n*) with artificial harmonics (*ah*), except for the last three notes, which are all artificial harmonics:

```
n  ah  n  ah  n  ah  n  ah  ah  ah
4   6  3   5  2   4  1   3   2   1
```

"TURKISH" FINGERSTYLE

In **Ex. 5.2** (Track 58), let's put down the pick and play with the fingers for four choruses of "Turkish Coffee 2000." The first pass is the melody chorus; the final two bars (11–12) are the "Turkish" phrase. The second and third choruses feature single-note improvisation with some chords interspersed. The goal here is to stay interesting for more than one chorus, using techniques like call and response to avoid unwanted repetition.

In the original version, the chords used in the melody were all quarter-notes. In this version the chords are basically the same, but the rhythm is sometimes changed to dotted-eighth/16th-notes to make it swing—see, for example, bar 1, beat 1, of the first chorus. The next measure starts a pattern of dotted-eighth/ 16ths where the 16th, a bass note, is tied to the next dotted-eighth chord. The aim of the rhythmic variation is to keep the swing without being monotonous. We also break things up rhythmically with space, like the last 16th-note of bar 5 where the *Gm7* stops short, or the staccato-like eighth-note chords in bar 7.

The single-note improvisation starts at bar 13, using the thumb. The line works through *E* minor in bar 13 to *A* minor to *A♯* diminished (bar 14), then back to the *E* minor. The last three notes of bar 15 then anticipate the *B♭m7* to *E♭9* in measure 16. Next, the line follows the chromatically descending minor sevenths in bars 17–18 and returns to *E* minor in bar 19. Now the 1st and 2nd fingers of the right hand are added to catch the chords starting with the last 16th-note of bar 19 through the first half of bar 21. After a quarter-rest, the single-note line resumes with the triplets (bar 21, beat 4), going to the second half of the third beat of bar 23, where the chords (starting with the *C♯13*) come in to finish the chorus.

The next chorus (bar 25) begins with chords and sets up a call and response: between the chords for a measure and a single-note line for a measure. The call with the chords (two measures this time) starts again in bar 27 and goes through 28, and the response, a variation on the "Turkish" melody, takes up three measures.

At measure 32, the single-note line anticipates measure 33's *F♯m7♭5* with a three-against-four phrase that you play by thumbing the first note of the group of 16ths (starting with the *B* of the 7th fret, 6th string) and hammering on the next two. Follow the accents—those are the thumb strokes.

Measure 34 uses a *C* jazz minor arpeggio to play the V7 chord, and the turnaround is basically *E* minor pentatonic—notice that in bar 35 the single-note line drops in an open 4th string on the second beat in anticipation of the *C♯m7♭5* that comes one beat later.

Ex. 5.2

First Three Choruses "Turkish" Fingerstyle

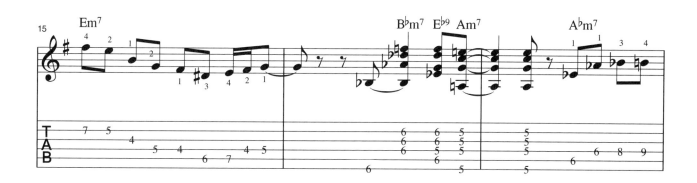

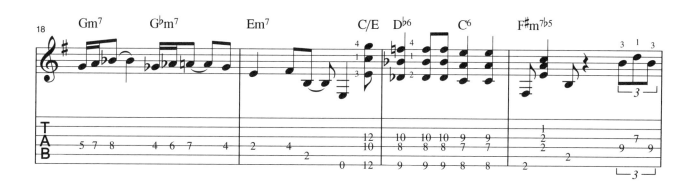

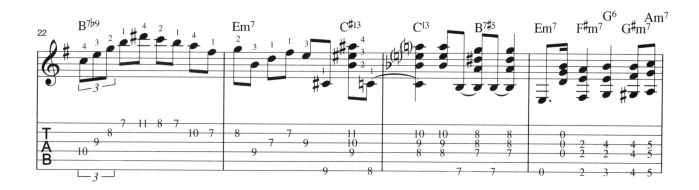

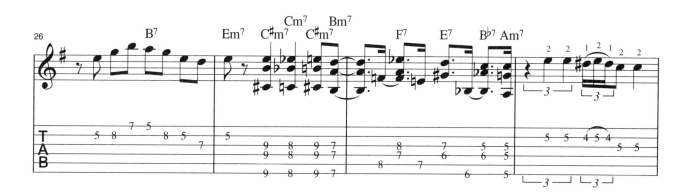

Ex. 5.3 (Track 59), the fourth chorus, departs from single-line improvisation and works only with chords until bars 11–12. One way to vary the chords-only approach is to play some low chords, as in the first four bars, then switch to a slightly higher register, as in bars 5–7. Then you can move to an in-between register, as in bars 8–10. Note the voicing called *F#m7b5* in bar 8 moves up a minor third in the same measure, but it is called *B7#5#9*, not *Am7b5*. In an ensemble situation, on that second chord, the bass would be playing a *B*, not *A*.

Ex. 5.3 **Fourth Chorus "Turkish Coffee 2000"**

The swift passage on the turnaround (bars 11–12) is a group of 16th-note augmented arpeggios played with the feel of quarter-note triplets. Here's where playing with the right-hand fingers comes in handy: you just go thumb–index–middle–ring, thumb–index–middle–ring, etc. This could be played with a pick, but the whole purpose here is to perform a solo piece without it (except for the artificial harmonics in the intro).

THE RIPPLE EFFECT

Our final piece expands the use of the right hand in the fingerstyle and adds two kinds of harmonics as well as the occasional use of the left-hand thumb. All these approaches should expand your options when you're looking for something different.

"Transparence," **Ex. 5.4** (Page 68; Tracks 60–61), is done almost entirely in the style of artificial harmonics alternating with normal notes—a ripple effect. The middle section is played fingerstyle, then we return to the ripple effect for the rest of the piece (the "return" is not transcribed here).

To get started, look at measure 1, the 12/8 bar. It starts with an artificial harmonic on an *A*: the 14th fret of the 3rd string (one octave higher than the fretted note) is the touch point. The next note, *G* (3rd fret, 1st string), is picked with an upstroke of the right-hand pinky fingernail. The *F#* that follows that *G* is a left-hand pull-off.

The next three notes in measure 1, *E–D–B,* consist of an artificial harmonic on *E* (14th fret, 4th string), a normal *D* note on the 2nd string, and another artificial harmonic on the *B* (14th fret, 5th string).

Next, the pinky plays the normal *A* (2nd fret, 3rd string), followed by an artificial *D* harmonic at the 12th fret, 6th string. Then the pinky plays the normal *A* note again, followed by an artificial harmonic on *B* (14th fret, 5th string), a normal *D* (like before, on the 2nd string), and back to the *E* artificial harmonic (14th fret, 4th string) to complete the measure.

Measure 2, in 6/8, is the same as the first six notes of the first measure. The next bar goes back to 12/8 and starts with a normal *A* (2nd fret, 3rd string), followed by an artificial harmonic touched at the 9th fret of the 3rd string in order to get the fifth degree (*E*) above the octave. (If you stayed with the same *A* at the 2nd fret, 3rd string, and played the artificial harmonic at the 7th fret, you'd get an *A* two octaves above the fretted note.)

This is the basic pattern of the ripple effect section. The piece goes through a major-sounding section for the first ten bars. Then at measure 11 there is a minor variation, which is a bit tricky, but if you follow the tab and listen to the CD, you can clarify the note sequence. Measure 19 has double octaves, all artificial harmonics. First you play the *B* on the 19th fret, 1st string, which is the same as a natural harmonic on the 7th fret, 1st string. From there you go to a point where frets 25 on the 2nd string and 24 on the 1st string would be. You have to experiment to find the exact location on your guitar where those double octaves ring out clearly.

The major section returns at bar 20. We have a pull-off variation in bars 25–26, then in bar 27 the last note, a *B,* has as its touch point the 9th fret of the 4th string. This note is the fifth between the octave *E* that goes up from the touch point at the 14th fret, 4th string, and the one at the 7th fret. Then you move your right hand over, in measure 28, to the corresponding fifths: *A*

(10th fret, 2nd string), *E* (9th fret, 3rd string), *D* (10th fret, first string), and *C#* (9th fret, 1st string). Next, move the right hand to the 7th fret of the 4th string to get the high *E,* and stay in the same position to get high *D, A, G,* and *F#* on strings 2, 3, and 1. Each touch point is five frets above the left hand, which has not moved from the second position since bar 22.

The fingerstyle playing starts at measure 30. The fingering below the notes is for the right hand, with the thumb written as *p* for *pulgar* (Spanish for thumb) and the other fingers as 1 for the index, 2 for the middle, and 3 for the ring (no pinky). The ring finger is used twice in a row in bars 30, 32, 34, and 36.

The last note of measure 31, the high *E,* is a natural harmonic, but it's played with the artificial harmonic technique: the index finger touches the 24th fret point on the 1st string and the ring finger plucks.

Beginning at measure 34 we have a series of barre chords moving down chromatically from the 6th fret to the 3rd (bar 37). In measure 38, the 3rd finger gets the *F#* on the sixth string, and you barre the 2nd fret over strings 4 through 2—that's the first half of the measure. Then your 3rd finger, still on the sixth string, drops down a half-step while your second finger covers strings 3 and 2 at the 2nd fret to get the *F7#5* chord. Next, the 2nd finger lifts up at beat 11 to allow the 1st finger to play the C.

Barre the 1st fret at measure 39 to get the *Bbmaj7* and *Ebmaj7/9*. At the second half of bar 40, you start another group of barres culminating with natural harmonics at the end of bar 43. The next barre comes at measure 50; look at the fingering for how to handle the jump from that 7th-fret barre to a single-note *C* at the 13th fret, 2nd string. This opens the door into some improvised single notes interspersed with chords, supported by the low *D* pedal. Some of the lines draw from an *Ab* augmented arpeggio—bars 52 to 53, for example, and 57 into 60.

At bar 60 the line uses a *B* jazz minor scale starting at beat 7. Notice that the last chord of bar 62, the *E* diminished, has a major seventh interval (*D♯*), and the same maj7 occurs in the diminished chords that follow through measure 65. Also, the roots of the 13/9 chords in bar 64 and 65 are not played but implied. Plus, the *A♭♯11/D* in bars 66 and 78 has no fifth (*E♭*) or third (*C*).

At bar 80 the key changes into *D* minor with a series of arpeggios. In bar 88, use the thumb of the left hand to cover the 6th and 5th strings at the 1st fret to get the *E♭maj7*.

At bar 90 the melody (the top notes of the chords) goes up a minor third and down a half-step, up a minor third, down a half-step, etc., while the chords (stacks of fourths) ascend chromatically. It looks complicated, but it's rather easy. Finally, for those *A* eighth-notes bouncing off the *D* pedal in bar 92, tap at the 7th fret with your right-hand middle finger and pull off (gently) to the open 6th string.

I did not include the entire transcription from the recording. What is transcribed here is enough, in my view, for anyone who really wants to work on these additional techniques. (Music begins on next page.)

Ex. 5.4

"Transparence"

CD Tracks 60-61

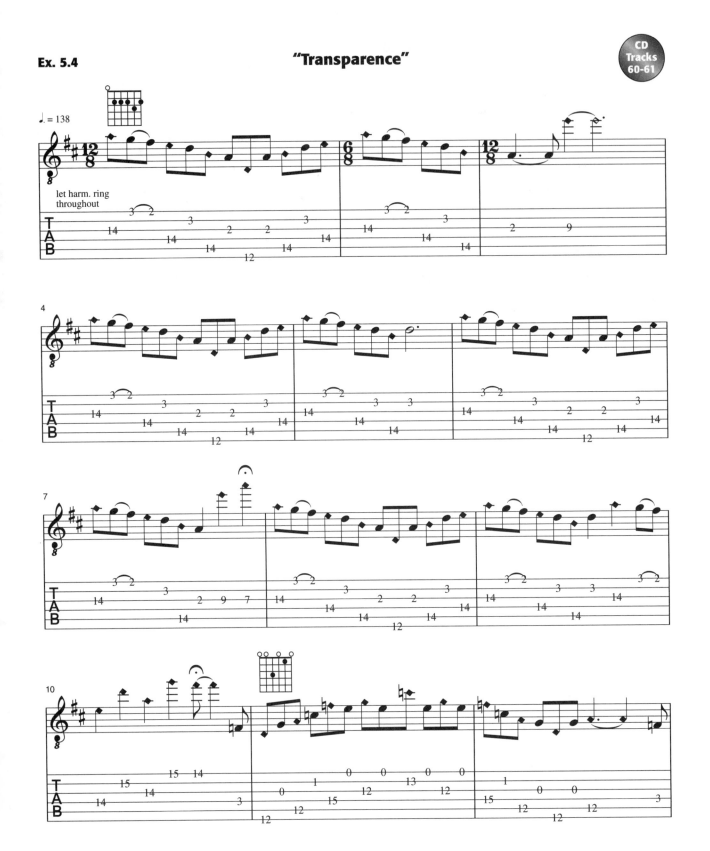

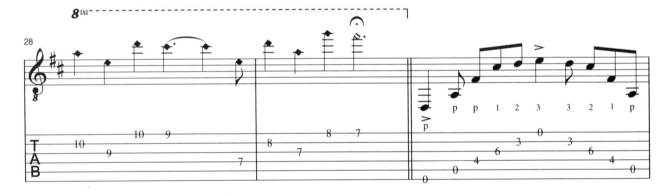

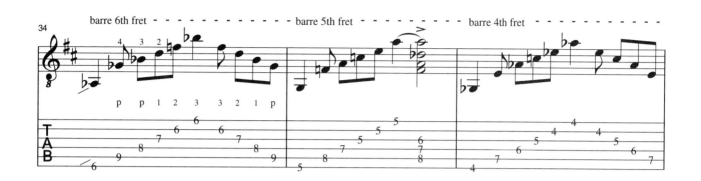

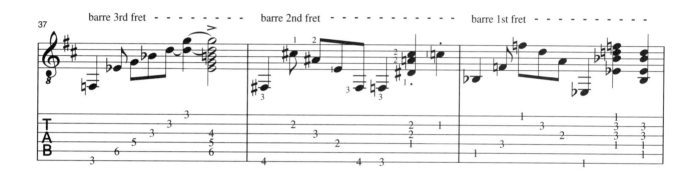

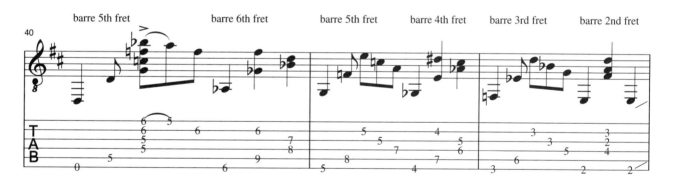

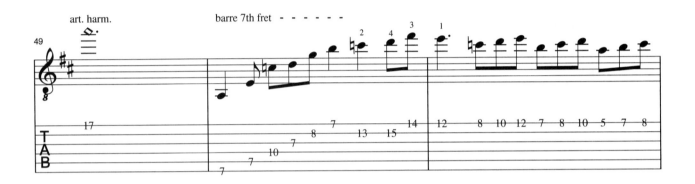

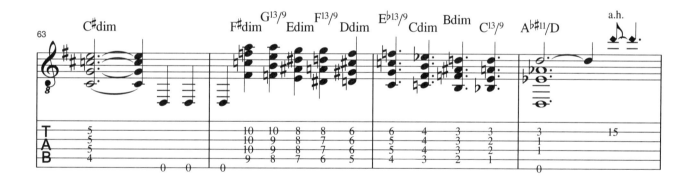
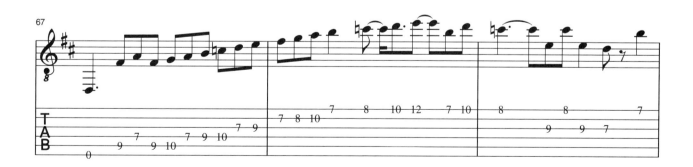

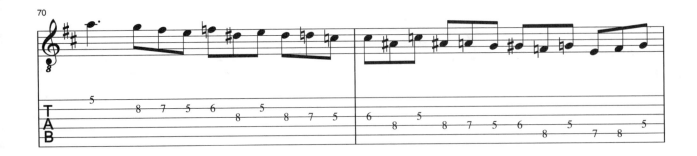

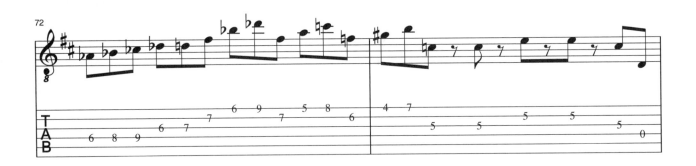

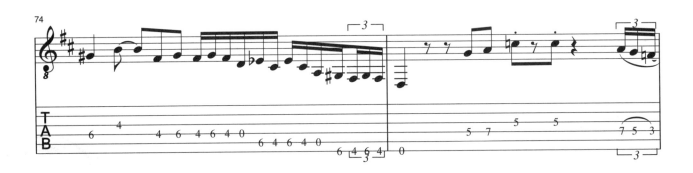

70
72
74
76
bend
F9sus4
E7add4
E♭9sus4
A♭♯11/D

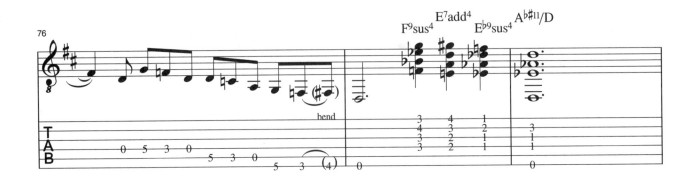

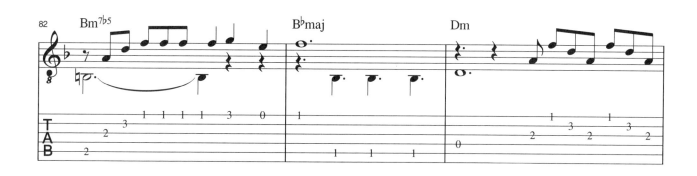

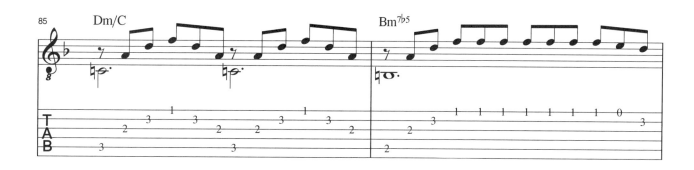

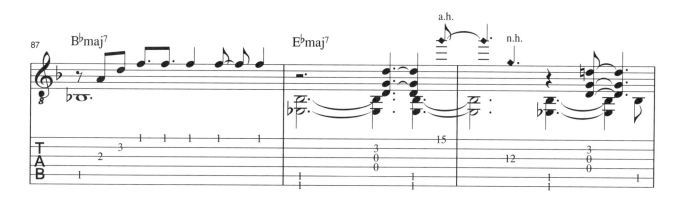

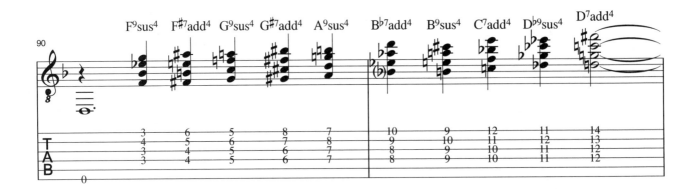

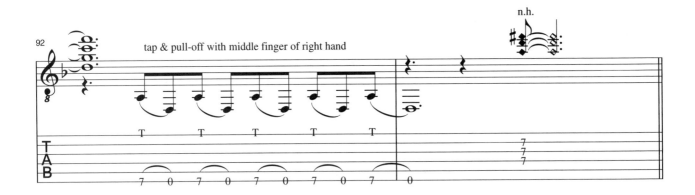

PARTING THOUGHTS

Beyond the techniques and ideas in this book, there are, of course, many aspects of improvising and playing music in general that need to be taught. However, I have seen that a lot of intangibles—things I mentioned in the introduction about using space, for example—need to be learned elsewhere.

For me that "elsewhere" has been on the bandstand, with great musicians and mentors—and it's a continuing thing, not just something that you need in your first few years of playing. One recent experience comes to mind. In 1990, I went on tour as a sideman for Wayne Shorter, a very special musician who truly walks to the beat of a different drum. A decade later I listened to a board-mix recording of one of our concerts in Italy. I thought some of the stuff I played was OK, but also I could hear I was trying to grab a quality from Wayne's music that was missing, or not fully developed, in my own playing. I discovered what that missing quality was a few weeks ago, when I was performing and Wayne happened to be in the audience. Afterward he told me, "You were very relaxed up there." That was it. I realized at the time I was in his group I lacked a more relaxed—not laid back, but relaxed—way of playing. Under his tutelage, I subconsciously picked up something I needed.

I have also noticed, when listening critically to recordings I've been on over the years, a welcome tendency to not blast into multi-note overdrive so much. I'm hearing more continuity in the lines, and (when playing with the right rhythm section) more skill in knowing where the time is in a piece, no matter how "out" I may go at certain points (this is related to what we worked on in Examples 4.3 and 4.4). Plus I feel I'm getting better, as I mentioned in the introduction, at using space in its many permutations. But there's more progress to be made—that's a requisite in this music.

My experience in music up to this point makes me sure that the things I share in these pages will help other players. So go back through this book, skip around, or go straight through again, looking for ideas that will help you get out of any ruts you're in or plateaus you're trying to transcend.

And do it with intensity, but be relaxed as well.

And remember that "wrong" may actually be right.

Do your best.

SELECTED DISCOGRAPHY

AS A LEADER

Free Spirit [ABC]
Coryell [Vanguard]
Spaces [Vanguard]
Fairyland [Mega]
Barefoot Boy [One Way]
Offering [Vanguard]
Introducing Larry Coryell
  & the 11th House [Vanguard]
Restful Mind [Vanguard]
Planet End [Vanguard]
Aspects [Arista]
The Lion and the Ram [Arista]
Twin House [Atlantic]
Two for the Road [Arista]
Standing Ovation [Mood]
Tributaries [Jive/Novus]
Splendid [Elektra]
Bolero [Evidence]
A Quiet Day in Spring [Steeple Chase]
L'oiseau De Feu (Firebird)/Petrouchka
  [Philips]
Together [Concord Jazz]
Le Sacre du Printemps [Philips]
American Odyssey [DRG]
Shining Hour [Muse]
Coryell Plays Ravel & Gershwin
  [Soundscreen]
Twelve Frets to One Octave [Shanachie]
Live from Bahia [Rhino]
Spaces Revisited [Shanachie]
Major Jazz Minor Blues [32 Jazz]
Monk, 'Trane, Miles & Me [High Note]
Private Concert [Acoustic Music]
The Coryells [Chesky]
New High [High Note]
Inner Urge [High Note]

Count's Jam Band Reunion [Tone Center]
Bolero/Scheherazade [Philips]

COMPILATIONS

Air Dancing [Jazzpoint]

WITH OTHERS

Chico Hamilton, ***The Dealer*** [Impulse!]
Gary Burton, ***Duster*** [Koch]
Gary Burton & Carla Bley, ***A Genuine Tong***
  Funeral [RCA]
The Jazz Composer's Orchestra,
  Communications [ECM]
Randy Brecker, ***Score*** [Blue Note]
Jim Pepper, ***Pepper's Pow Wow*** [Atlantic]
Herbie Mann, ***Memphis Underground***
  [Atlantic]
Lenny White, ***Venusian Summer***
  [Wounded Bird]
Charles Mingus, ***Three or Four Shades***
  of Blues [Atlantic]
Charles Mingus, ***Me, Myself an Eye***
  [Atlantic]
Sonny Rollins, ***Don't Ask*** [OJC]
Stephane Grappelli, ***Young Django***
  [Polygram]
Michael Mantler, ***Movies*** [Virgin]
Stu Goldberg, ***Solos Duos Trio*** [MPS]
Paco de Lucia, ***Castro Marin*** [Polygram]
L. Subramaniam, ***From the Ashes*** [Waterlily]
Steve Marcus, ***Count's Rock Band/Lord's***
  Prayer [Collectables]
Ronu Majumdar, Abhijit Banerjee, Keyvan
  Chemirani, ***Moonlight Whispers*** [TIM]
Hariprasad Chaurasia, ***Music Without***
  Boundaries [Navras]

Serious Players.

The Music Player Network is for serious players. From guitars, bass, keyboards and recording to computer music culture, dance, trance and more. • Our industry-leading magazines, *Guitar Player, Keyboard, Bass Player, Gig, MC², Rumble, EQ* and *Extreme Groove*, take the art of playing music seriously. And so does our leading portal website, MusicPlayer.com. • Our editors and writers are experienced musicians and engineers with special insights and hands-on experience that only comes from real-time playing. • If you want to get serious about your playing, check us out at your nearest newsstand or visit MusicPlayer.com on the web.

WHEN IT COMES TO GUITARS, WE WROTE THE BOOK.

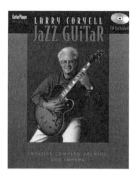

Jazz Guitar
Creative Comping, Soloing, and Improv
By Larry Coryell

This workbook/CD set challenges advanced guitarists to heighten creativity, increase flexibility, expand jazz vocabulary, and brighten playing style. Al DiMeola says it "opens the door to a better understanding in our quest for advanced guitar playing."
Softcover with CD, 96 pages, ISBN 0-87930-550-9, $19.95

Jaco
The Extraordinary and Tragic Life of Jaco Pastorius
By Bill Milkowski

This biography has become the classic portrait of the troubled genius who revolutionized modern electric bass. Featuring reminiscences from artists who played with him, it reveals how Jaco played melodies, chords, harmonics and percussive effects simultaneously, while fusing jazz, classical, R&B, rock, reggae, pop, and punk—all before age 35, when he met his tragic death.
Softcover, 263 pages, ISBN 0-87930-426-X, $14.95

How To Make Your Electric Guitar Play Great!
By Dan Erlewine

This "owner's manual" covers everything you need to choose, use, and improve any electric guitar—and to get the best sound for your own playing style. It examines assessing construction and price; tools and techniques; personalizing action, intonation, and tuning; electronics; and more. Includes a handy plastic sheet of punch-out radius gauges.
Softcover, 133 pages, ISBN 0-87930-601-7, $17.95

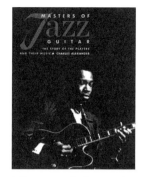

Masters of Jazz Guitar
The Story of the Players and their Music
Edited by Charles Alexander

The guitar is fundamental to jazz, and has created its own legacy of greatness over the years. This handsome and insightful book honors the lives, work, and far-reaching influences of virtuoso jazz guitarists past and present, such as Django Reinhardt, Charlie Christian, Wes Montgomery, Joe Pass, Pat Metheny, and dozens more.
Hardcover, 176 pages, ISBN 0-87930-592-4, $39.95

Grant Green
Rediscovering the Forgotten Genius of Jazz Guitar
Sharony Andrews Green

This heartfelt biography celebrates the brief life and brilliant music of the late jazz guitarist Grant Green, whose legend still grows today. Best known as a Blue Note Records session leader and sideman in the 1960s, Green's aggressive but eloquent tones embraced bebop, hard bop, blues, soul, gospel, Latin, country, pop, and funk.
Softcover, 274 pages, IBSN 0-87930-698-X, $16.95

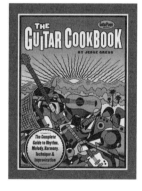

The Guitar Cookbook
By Jesse Gress

This user-friendly guide helps beginning, intermediate, and advanced players in any genre understand the mechanisms of music on the guitar. These "recipes" unlock the logic of the fingerboard with hundreds of musical examples and concepts. You'll increase rhythmic, melodic and harmonic awareness, develop a personalized vocabulary, and discover fresh techniques that make your playing sizzle.
Softcover, 244 pages, ISBN 0-87930-633-5, $24.95

Backbeat Books

AVAILABLE AT FINE BOOK AND MUSIC STORES EVERYWHERE. OR CONTACT:
Backbeat Books • 6600 Silacci Way • Gilroy, CA 95020 USA
Phone: Toll free (866) 222-5232 • Fax: (408) 848-5784
E-mail: backbeat@rushorder.com • **Web:** www.backbeatbooks.com